FROM THE GUTTERMOST TO THE UTTERMOST

From the Guttermost to the Uttermost

From a Biblical Perspective

Rev. Dr. Laurie McDonald

authorHOUSE®

AuthorHouse™
1663 Liberty Drive
Bloomington, IN 47403
www.authorhouse.com
Phone: 1-800-839-8640

First published by AuthorHouse   01/21/2012

ISBN: 978-1-4685-4612-5 (sc)
ISBN: 978-1-4685-4613-2 (ebk)

Library of Congress Control Number: 2012901296

Printed in the United States of America

Any people depicted in stock imagery provided by Thinkstock are models, and such images are being used for illustrative purposes only.
Certain stock imagery © Thinkstock.

This book is printed on acid-free paper.

Because of the dynamic nature of the Internet, any web addresses or links contained in this book may have changed since publication and may no longer be valid. The views expressed in this work are solely those of the author and do not necessarily reflect the views of the publisher, and the publisher hereby disclaims any responsibility for them.

CONTENTS

ACKNOWLEDGEMENT

I would like to thank my husband, Dr. Osofo L. H. McDonald for his patience and support as I pursue God's best for me. Also my sister Jackie and other siblings, as well as my 10 children, Sheila (RN), Michael (BA, Teacher), Donna (MS, Psychologist), Leslie (LVN), Marc (BA, JD), Z Ukoni (AS, Active in LA), T Star (Artist, Cosmotologist), Donald (BA in Biology), Tyme (Marine & Army retired), and Laurie (BA Psychology), who lived through this with me. I am proud of all of you.

INTRODUCTION

At last, I have taken pen in hand to write my autobiography. People have told down through the years, "You should write your story", but I was always too busy, but the time has arrived to complete the book. I know now that it wasn't time to write the story until I had grown some and some of the characters died. Even though I mention no names, it is not hard to imagine who I am talking about if you know me. My children used to be ashamed when I gave my testimony in church of my deliverance, but now that they are adult, I have their blessing to tell the story.

How can God change a prostitute into a pastor? For forty-five years I have been testifying of the miracle of God's grace, this is the story of the process, with its highs and lows. I knew the name of the book from the beginning but I had to live it out to prove that it can be done. "From the Guttermost to the Uttermost is one woman's story of deliverance

As the title suggests, I believe God has brought me from the lowest level of life to the highest. The definition for gutter is **of worst kind:**of the most vulgar, corrupt, or morally degraded kind. The definition of uttermost is **greatest degree or amount:** number, or amount of something, especially the greatest effort that somebody is capable of. There is a scripture in the bible that states "Wherefore he is able also to save them to the uttermost that comes unto God by him, seeing he ever liveth to make intercession for them." (Hebrews

7:25 KJV). Jesus ability to save reaches to the uttermost depths of guilt and depravity; the greatest sinners can be saved. He is able to lift us higher than we ever have been by seating us in heavenly places in Christ Jesus. (Ephesians 2:6)

This passage of scripture is talking about Jesus being our Great High Priest who, contrary to the Aaronic priesthood of the Old Testament, is able to deliver us completely (justified), entirely (sanctified), and eternally (glorified). My deliverance is not my own doing. I didn't turn over a new leaf, pull myself up by my own bootstraps, or get a new attitude. I had an encounter with the Living God through Jesus Christ our Eternal high Priest. My life has been changed forever, and this book is written to give someone hope for their deliverance, and to give glory to God. I have read other books that seemed to glorify sin to make the book more interesting. I find nothing pleasant or exciting about the sin that took my Savior to the cross. Some may read it out of curiosity and others may read it for information. My greatest desire in writing this book is that someone reading it might avoid some of the pitfalls, learn from my mistakes, and above find the God who can save anybody.

PART 1

THE EARLY YEARS

LIVING WITH SHAME

If a child lives with criticism, he learns to condemn, If a child lives with hostility, he learns to fight. If a child lives with ridicule, he learns to feel shy. If a child lives with shame, he learns to feel guilty. If a child lives with tolerance, he learns to be patient. If child lives with encouragement, he learns confidence. If a child lives with praise, he learns to appreciate. If a child lives with fairness, he learns justice. If a child lives with security, he learns to have faith. If a child lives with approval, he learns to like himself. If a child lives with acceptance and friendship, he learns to find love in the world. (*Author: Dorothy Law Neite*)

If children in this stage are encouraged and supported in their increased independence, they become more confident and secure in their own ability to survive in the world. If children are criticized, overly controlled, or not given the opportunity to assert themselves, they begin to feel inadequate in their ability to survive, and may then become overly dependent upon others, lack self-esteem, and feel a sense of shame or doubt in their own abilities.(1)

God spoke to Jeremiah in the first chapter of the book named after him, saying "Before I formed you in the womb I knew you; before you were born I sanctified you; I ordained you a prophet to the nations." This is the case in all of our lives, He chooses the family, the circumstance, and the time of our birth, and at some particular time He calls us to Himself and begins to shape us into His image.

I heard that I was born in a house in Watts, California in 1945. I was the third of ten children of my mother. "Can any good thing come out of Watts, or Compton?" was a common colloquial. I was bathed in the kitchen sink, after they unwrapped my navel cord from around my neck and cut it. My mother said I was born hungry because the nutrients could not properly be received because of the position of the naval cord. I do recall a deep hunger both physical and spiritual. There was no closeness with my mother, so I went about to earn this love which should have been natural. My father, a want-to-be-boxer, was absent most of the time, he would hang out at the "Ice House" around the corner with his friends or he would be in "Road Camp" where the county sent indigent fathers for child support issues. Once, when he was in "Road Camp," he sent my sister and me a small "covered wagon" with our names inscribed on them. He would give us a dollar on our birthday, and once I recall, he hugged me in the kitchen, and I felt loved. I don't remember any moments like this with my mother until I was an adult.

"Children's children are the crown of old men, and the glory of the children is their father."(Proverbs 17:6) My mother was there with me as I grew up, but my father had been enshrined in my heart even though I hardly saw him. Fathers play an awesome role in the child's development and when the father does not know who he is, the child has no identity. Mothers are the nurturers but you cannot nurture what is not there.

When I was seven years old, my mother went in to labor with her eighth child, and I was the only one around. She told me "Go down to the Ice House and tell Daddy, "This is it!" I ran down to the corner where Daddy and his friends were; hair uncombed, no shoes, dirty dress, and said "Momma said this is it!" I remember his face, he was ashamed.

I was ashamed too. At school, the teacher noticed that my dress was dirty and she decided to take it off and wash if for me. (Back in the day they could do things like that.) She found a large brown bag that was used to cover clothes from the cleaners; she enlarged the hole in the top for my head and put it on me. I could not sit down because it would tear, so she let me paint on an easel in front of the class while my dress dried on the radiator-like heater. I was ashamed but I learned to live with it. I recall being hungry at school (that was before free breakfast) and I would pretend I was throwing paper in the waste basket in class, so I could retrieve half eaten candy or chewing gum out of the trash. I began to get in trouble in class and was sent to the cloak room for punishment, while there I would search all of the pockets for money or candy.

My mother needed a lot help because she was always pregnant or tired. I seemed to be the designated helper or I was always trying to prove myself worthy of love. I recall the day, around age seven, the coffee pot was burning on the stove, and my younger sister and I raced to the kitchen to turn it off. I picked up the coffee pot and accidently scalded my sister on her chest. She screamed to highest heaven and I ran into the living room to explain. Momma was upset and grabbed a lamp, intending to whip me with the extension cord, but I was squirming so much she broke the lamp on my leg and made a big hole. The ambulance came and Momma told me to say that the lamp fell on me while I was getting a whipping. I was compliant, but I never forgot, and the sixteen stiches I received didn't let me forget.

We were born in an era where switches, extension cords and belts were the order of the day for disciplining children. Parents did to their children what was done to them. The scripture that was quoted was Proverbs 23:13-14 "Withhold not correction from the child; for if thou beatest him with a rod, he shall not die. Thou shalt beat him with a rod, and deliver his soul from hell." Today, you can only spank a child with your open palm on his/her buttocks. In fact, any suspicious marks on a child are taken in to consideration when a child is brought to the hospital. Parents are no longer empowered to discipline and the result is children running the society and confusion everywhere.

At age eight, right after Valentine's Day, I had remembered the candy my mother received from my step-father and I went into their bedroom and tried to reach it on a shelf but it fell down and spilled under the bed. I took a match and lit a string hanging down from the mattress under the bed and found the candy, but forgot all about the string burning. I left the room and before long the entire house was on fire, the Red Cross came to provide clothes and food, and we had to move to my great aunt's other house. We were in the newspaper with the heading "Mother of Eight, House Burns" of course I told no one until years later. Even after moving to the house behind my great aunt's house, I still played with fire, but this time I only burned down the garage.

After the last fire, my great aunt moved us to Delano, to another house she owned. She was the matriarch of the family. She had fallen down one day in her kitchen and broke her hip and so she always had her crutch with her. She handled my mother's welfare check, and brought us food whenever the check came. My mother did not drive, or work as she only had an eighth grade education. She was an only child herself and did not have many life skills such as cooking and cleaning. So my great-aunt took my brother, and he stayed with them, my aunt who lived across the street took my younger sister to live with her and her husband. Each summer I would look forward to staying with my grandmother who lived in Los Angeles.

There was of course sibling rivalry because my older sister had rheumatic fever as a child which caused her to get special attention. We would vie for our mother's attention but it was impossible for her to love us all with no guidance or preparation for such a large family. My oldest sister was already going out with boys before we left Delano, and the next sister had been sickly and was spoiled.

That left me to clean up the house or cook whenever Mama needed help or I wanted to go somewhere.

It was my grandmother who came over and made us clean-up, and my great aunt who handled all of our money. My great aunt was a business woman, who owned houses, ran a barbecue business, and a hotel. Someone called it a brothel where farmers could come and do-whatever with the women. I don't know, but she would have my sisters and I clean it up and we would find thongs (panties) before they were popular. I have often wondered if this was when that spirit of prostitution came up on us, since all of us eventually chose that profession.

It was not long after we moved to Delano, when I was ten years old, that my father died of cirrhosis of the liver. I was devastated; he seemed to genuinely love me even though I did not see him much. Uncle Otis was my step-father but he drank a lot like my father, so he and my mother were always fighting and he eventually left. I loved living in the country; we could pick cotton and watermelons to earn money to go to the show. We made friends with a family whose father was a contractor for laborers and we could work for him whenever we wanted to earn money. Life was carefree in the country for a while as we enjoyed walking through the fields and making up our own games.

My mother took us to a Holy Ghost church where the people clapped and shouted to the music. My sisters and I were asked to sing songs and we formed a little group. The church was a place of refuge for our family because they would help us with the things we needed when they could. I liked church even though I did not understand it. I recall that our aunt requested that we get baptized in a Baptist church which she attended. She went to church on Sundays but she would cuss people out when she was angry and even hit you with her crutch.

My mother was in her early thirties with black hair (she was half-American Indian), she had eight children and no husband. It wasn't long before she became friends with our next door neighbor. Soon he began coming over and going in the bedroom with my mom. He was a sixty-five year old Hispanic man who had a house next door, with chickens, goats, and other farm animals. My mother had gained weight but was still attractive. The man began to watch television with us in the living room, while momma was sleep in the bedroom. He began to put his hand under the cover we had over us on the couch. That was the beginning; soon momma would ask me to go over to his house to get milk or sugar. The man would lay me down on the kitchen floor to perform oral sex on me. Eventually, he would come to the school to pick me up and then lay me down in the seat. He would give me fifty cents and say "Don't tell Rosa!"

Picture of Mama

I could buy a Boston cream pie with that money and that was the beginning of taking money for favors. It did not hurt except for the prickly beard. I guess he could do no more than that. I attempted to tell my mother once when I saw him looking in my little sister's panties, but she did not believe me, and I was ashamed that I let him do it. This lasted for a while even though my mother had two children by him; I had to try to stay away from him because he was always trying to get me. By now I had a crush on a boy at school, but I felt inferior and I guess it showed. I would fall hard for a boy but sooner or later I was rejected. It was during this time I graduated from eighth grade to ninth. I was asked to say a speech for the graduation and I don't remember having support from my family. It was noticeable even then that I had the ability to stand before an audience.

I was glad to leave Delano at first because I could get away from my shame, but once I returned to homesteaded house in Watts where I had been born, I missed my friends, and before long caught the grey hound bus all by myself and went back to Delano to see my friends. In a few days I had to go back and face the new life as a teenager in Watts.

PART 2

THE TEEN YEARS

No Where to Run

During adolescence, the transition from childhood to adulthood is most important. Children are becoming more independent, and begin to look at the future in terms of career, relationships, families, housing, etc. This is a major stage in development where the child has to learn the roles he will occupy as an adult. It is during this stage that the adolescent will re-examine his identity and try to find out exactly who he is. Erikson suggests that two identities are involved: the sexual and the occupational. Erikson claims that the adolescent may feel uncomfortable about their body for a while until they can adapt and "grow into" the changes. Success in this stage will lead to the virtue of **fidelity**.(2)

When we arrived at the old homestead in Watts (where I had been born) I had never noticed how small it was until we arrived with nine children (mama was pregnant). The ages were 17 (sister), 14 (sister), 13 (me), 11 (sister), 9 (brother), 8 (sister), 7 sister, 6 brother, and 2 (brother). It may have been one or two bedrooms, so most of the time we slept together. This was a time when young girls are blossoming and we are excited about the newness of life. We were still on welfare and since my great-aunt died; my grandmother was there to assist my mother through the pregnancy. Mama always found a church and we knew we would have to go with her. I began to want to go out and be with other teenagers and so I would finish my work early on Friday nights so I could go to the Hunter Hancock

Record Hop. I grew up with the songs of Motown with which I identified songs like "Bad Girl" by the Miracles and "No Where to Run", and I loved music and dancing. I didn't care if I had to make 100 tacos (it felt like 100) and clean the whole house, I would do anything to get to the Record Hop. I didn't have nice clothes, but everybody looked alright when the party lights were on.

I remember one night I had finished all my work and was planning to go out but mama found something that was not done right and I was told I could not go. I remember going into the bedroom and climbing out of the window. I did not think of the consequences, I just had to go. I adopted an attitude that if I did not like something I would leave. I stayed out that night over a girl friend's house but her mother became concerned the next day and sent me home. I went to Juvenile Hall and stayed a few days and was released back home. I had lost the ability to submit to authority. My grades were dropping all of the time as school no longer interested me. I would ditch with my friends and eventually started experimenting with drugs. Someone was smoking marijuana and I asked if I could try it. All I can remember of that episode is that I had a hallucination where people began to look like robot policemen. It was during those times of going to house parties and getting "high' that I lost my virginity.

I was out of control and my mother could no longer count on me coming home at night. I remember one night I almost did not make it home because I had taken some pills and began to stagger down the street and a man pulled a knife on me and took me to a vacant lot and did what he wanted. I could have been stabbed or killed but God was merciful to me and somehow I made it home. It may have been on a night like this that mama placed me back in Juvenile Hall.

This time the juvenile authorities sent me to a Foster Home and I tried to follow their rules. I just didn't like the people and so I left. I wasn't afraid to go back to Juvenile because I had some friends that were just like me; mixed up and confused. They gave me a nickname "Desperate" because I said the word all of the time. I identified with these misfits when I heard their tales of molestation and abandonment by their families. I put tattoos on me by taking the lead from a pencil and a needle and writing on my arms and legs. I began to be attracted to girls because that was the mindset of the environment. It started off with affairs of the heart until once when I was released I tried the lesbian life and found it as empty as the heterosexual life. Life is always empty when you try to live without God. The bible states that people who reject God "Changed the truth of God into a lie, and worshipped and served the creature more than the creator, who is blessed forever. For this cause God gave them up unto vile affections; for even the women did change the natural use into that which is against nature; and likewise also the men, leaving the natural use of the woman; burned in their lust one toward another; men with men working that which is unseemly (indecent) and receiving in themselves the recompense (the inevitable consequences and penalty) of their error which was meet (their fitting reward)." Molestation and rape are not valid excuses to violate the word of God. He is a deliverer and if you desire to be saved he will save you completely or to the uttermost.

After running away from at least 3 Foster Homes the authorities decided to put me with my grandmother. She was willing to give her little granddaughter some help, but even my grandmother's love could not help me now. I eventually ended up at South Park, where my sisters and their friends were hanging out. There was a hamburger stand across from the park and in the evening we would go there to eat and dance. The guys had their malt liquor and their wine. I was 15 years old and I met the young man I was going to marry. He was 16, muscular, funny, and somewhat handsome. He had a lot of heart and was not afraid of anyone. His father had been an alcoholic, but had recovered and remarried. His mother had mental health issues and I would hear her talking to herself especially when she was drinking. His older siblings were alienated from him and all he had was his beloved sister. She looked like him and when they were together they could keep you laughing. I saw him and began to follow him around. He told me he had a girlfriend and I responded "I am going to marry you and have your children."

Once we went over to one of his friend's house and he noticed that I kept going outside to check on something. He followed me and found that I had my clothes in a bag and that I had run away. His comment was "Aw Man," (his famous words). He then asked his sister if I could stay there. That's why I liked him; he was concerned about my welfare, not about what he could get. Soon, his mother moved out of the house where they were living and went to Santa Monica. He was left in an empty house because he didn't want to go with his mother and her boyfriend. I remember the day the police picked him up and took him away to Youth Authority, because he was living on his own and underage. I would continue to go over to his sister's house when I wasn't at the park. I felt like I was in love, each time I heard our song "Stand by Me" by Ben E. King, it brought back memories of him. He received a little more than a year and I was looking forward to him coming home again.

I ruined that relationship when I messed with a friend of his. This friend was older than us and he had recently gotten out of prison. He had light hazel eyes and I was attracted to him. I went to his house one day and that was a big mistake because he took advantage of the opportunity with a little force. It wasn't long before my boyfriend heard about it either from me or someone else. I had broken one of the codes of honor and I was never able to convince him I didn't mean to betray him.

I eventually moved back to my mother's house, and I was there when my boyfriend got out. He really wanted to move on, but I was persistent. We would hang out with his sister and her little son and before long I was pregnant. When I told my mother, she insisted we get married. In fact, it was mandatory, so she brought her pastor over and we were married when the baby was 2 months old. He got a job downtown as a delivery boy making $40 a week. That was enough to pay for a small kitchenette, buy food and leave enough for us to walk down to the show for the first few weeks. That was June and by the end of the year we were arguing. He complained that his legs were hurting from riding that bike, and the people treated him like a boy when he was a man. He would go to work in the morning and not get home until 2:00am in the morning. He would be drunk, talking about me and the friend that I had messed with; he even threw me and the baby out one night. He would go back to work and I would be there in the apartment all day, with no television or anything. I started sitting out on the balcony that looked over the street and on one of those days I met a young lady and her boyfriend. She said she was a model and her clothes gave the impression she had something. After one of those fights I told the young lady I would like to be a model too. I don't know if I left while he was sleep or waited until he left the next day, but I ran away again. Now I did not know this woman and did not desire to be with her boyfriend, but I had to get away.

The book of Proverbs is filled with admonitions regarding the strange woman (prostitute). In chapter 2:1-2 we find the warning to "Receive my words, and hide my commandments with thee; So that thou incline thine ear to wisdom and apply thine heart to understanding . . . . to deliver thee from the strange woman, even from the stranger which flattereth with her words; which forsaketh the guide of her youth, and forgetteth the covenant with her God." (Proverbs 2:16-17)

It seems the next day I found that she was not a model but a prostitute. I was neither afraid nor shocked, as she gave me pointers on how to pick the "date." Everything in my life up until now had prepared me for this. I did not value my body, and I decided if people put a value on it they would pay.

Soon my husband found where I was and he came and got the baby and took her to his father's house. His father and his step mother fell in love with our baby and she became their little princess. She remained with them for 2 years as I went from pimp to pimp and in and out of jail. More than once I escaped with my life when someone decided they could take what they wanted. I wasn't very smart because I spent 13 months in jail at various times and 9 months on the street. I was riding around in Cadillacs and living in Lemert Park acting as if I was living the high life, when all along I was being used to support someone else's life style. Nothing I had was my own. I did not do these things because I loved some man or because I was hooked on drugs, I did it because I did not value myself or my child.

"In the twilight, in the evening, in the black and dark of night; and behold, there met him a woman with the attire of an harlot, and subtle (cunning, crafty) of heart. (she is loud and stubborn; her feet abide not in her house; Now she is without, now in the streets, and lieth wait at every corner. (Proverbs 7:9-12)

I began to go jail and as soon as I was booked, I was out on bail so I could make more money. This left me without remorse, and I did not take it seriously. I served time eventually, but when I was released I went back. There was nowhere to run. The last time I was arrested, the judge decided to take the three cases I had and run them consecutively so that I would spend nearly a year in jail. This probably was the best thing for me at the time.

"And when he had spent all, there arose a mighty famine in the land; and he began to be in want. And he went and joined himself to a citizen of that country; and he sent into his fields to feed swine. And he would fain (desire) have filled his belly with the husks that the swine did eat; and no man gave unto him." (Luke 15:14-16). I was twenty years old, and the novelty of the life was gone. Many young girls have found themselves cast aside after they had followed a false promise of satisfaction and success.

PART 3

YOUNG ADULT

AN OPPORTUNITY FOR A NEW LIFE

In young adulthood, we begin to share ourselves more intimately with others. We explore relationships leading toward longer term commitments with someone other than a family member. Successful completion can lead to comfortable relationships and a sense of commitment, safety, and care within a relationship. Avoiding intimacy, fearing commitment and relationships can lead to isolation, loneliness, and sometimes depression.(3)

There I was sitting in jail, learning how to do time, without a letter or a visit. Mama always told us, if you go to jail; don't expect me to come up there. That was a good thing. My mind was confused with no vision for my future. Did I want I want to continue my pursuit of love wherever I could find it?

I had heard about a Gospel group that came to the jail from the Church of God in Christ on the third Sunday. I went to the auditorium on that third Sunday because it was one way to see your friends, and I wanted to see this group that everybody was talking about. I was not trying to find the Lord. I heard the songs and I watched the speaker as she waited to be presented. She kept looking up at the ceiling as if to worship God. She had a look on her face that made me desire what she had. I had been around people in church most of my life but I never felt anything. I knew my mother went to church, but I also knew her weakness. I thought she did not like me and I did not want to be like her. I don't know what was happening that day except God got my attention. Soon the speaker got up and she began to talk about a life that was being destroyed, and how Satan can cause you to become a degenerate and how you end up in destruction. She went on to talk about Jesus, and how he came to renew, restore and regenerate. I began to move around in the seat to see if she was looking at me. I was sure she saw me, I had not heard of the conviction of the Holy Spirit.

I did not know that God was calling me and everyone who would listen, and this woman was only a tool. She finished her message and I wanted to talk to her, but in jail there is no altar call, to avoid any emotional outbreaks and confusion. I was able to make an appointment with the Chaplain for the following Tuesday. I went to see the Chaplain and I remember her bewildered look when I said "I want what the lady was talking about." She said that is a good thought, just keep thinking like that and everything will be alright. I left the office feeling as if the Chaplain did not know what to do with me. But God did, I was released in a short while and went back to my last boyfriend/pimp. It was not long until "a voice" said in my heart, "You're living in adultery." I had never been concerned about adultery before but now I wanted to move out. Soon I got my own apartment and went to visit my daughter and they let her spend the night. That "Voice" came again as said "go back to your husband" and that was the last thing I wanted because I knew he would not let me live that life style down. I invited him over and we decided to try again. We moved back to the eastside to start all over again, and his father and step-mother reluctantly let us have our daughter. Not long after I was home with my husband the police came and picked me up because I had a case pending. This time I was pregnant and knew I had a home to go to when I was released. I remember one Sunday, about 3 months after the baby was born, I heard that "Voice" say "Go to Church" and I started preparing to go to a church around the corner, but the "Voice" inside said "Go to your mother's church."

I called my mother and she sent the pastor and his wife to pick me, my daughter and the baby up for church. They were a nice middle-aged couple who were very pious and conservative. I had seen them praying in the living room of my mother's home a few times, when my sister's and I were preparing to go out to the street. I did not know about the power of prayer and that I was a recipient of that power.

I was a little self-conscious, not having on stockings and I knew my clothing betrayed my profession, but I had not come for form or fashion, I came to find peace. When the pastor finished his message and gave the altar call, I got up and knelt down at the altar. The pastor's wife came beside me with an open bible in her hand and asked me if I wanted to be saved. I responded "Yes!" She took me to Roman's 3:23 and showed me that "All have sinned and come short of the glory of God." I felt better now that I knew everyone sinned. The pastor's wife then showed me Romans 6:23 where the bible read "The wages of sin is death but the gift of God is eternal life through Jesus Christ our Lord." I wanted this gift but I began to tell her I may have gone too far and maybe God would not accept me. She quickly turned to John 6:37 that read "All that the Father gives me will come to me, and him that comes to me I will in no wise cast out." I don't know why I believed this, perhaps, God gave me the faith to understand and believe because His word does say in Romans 10:17 "Faith comes by hearing and hearing by the word of God."

She then showed me the scripture in Romans 10:9-10 that said "if you shall confess with your mouth the Lord Jesus and believe in your heart that God has raised Him from the dead, you shall be saved." I said "I believe that" and she asked me to repeat this prayer after her. "Dear God, I know that I am a sinner according to your word, I have sinned against you and I now turn from my sin and confess with my mouth that Jesus is my Lord. Come into my heart Lord Jesus and forgive me of all of my sins. In Jesus name. Amen" She then showed me Revelation 3:20 which stated "Behold, I stand at the door and knock; if any man hear my voice, and open the door, I will come in to him, and will sup with him and him with me." She asked me where was Jesus now and I responded "He's in my heart." I knew from that point on I was saved, not because I felt different but because the word said I was saved. That was January 8th, 1967, the day I was born again. I went home from church and told my husband I was saved and his response was "Saved from what?" I thought he would be happy, but little did I know, the war had just begun.

My pastor and wife picked me up every Sunday and I sat in Sunday school and church. I was learning the teachings of Christ. My pastor taught that Jesus was God in human form and one of his favorite scriptures was 1 Timothy 3:16 "And without controversy great is the mystery of godliness; God was manifest in the flesh, justified in the Spirit, seen of angels, preached unto the gentiles, believed on in the world, received up into glory." I began to get up in church and give my testimony of how God delivered me and each time I told the story the church began to shout and I became more and more bold. I began to teach the toddler class because I had so many toddlers, and then I began to teach the primary class for the 1st grades. I just wanted to serve God. I saw people shouting and speaking in an unknown tongue and I wanted what they had. I would tarry at the altar and pray and cry until my throat was dry but I still didn't get filled with the Holy Ghost. Sometimes people would pray with me at the altar and they would say things like "Hold on, or "Let Go." I did not know what to do. I tried to be perfect but I just couldn't fill worthy enough for the Holy Spirit to come and fill me. One day I was reading my bible in Luke 11:11-13 and it read "If a son shall ask bread of any of you that is a father, will you give him a stone? Or if he asks a fish, will he for a fish give him a serpent? Or if he shall ask for an egg, will he give him a scorpion? If you then, being evil (born sinners) know how to give good gifts to your children; how much more will your heavenly Father give the Holy Spirit to them that ask Him?" That was enough for me, a few days later the pastor's wife and another missionary came over to pray with me and faith filled my heart and I stopped speaking in English and allowed the words that were in my heart to flow out of me and I was filled with the Holy Ghost, that was 1969, two years after I was saved. I had more boldness to speak God's word. I had power to witness and tell people everywhere I went about Jesus. I was not ashamed even if I was in a welfare line, I would pass out Christian tracts that said God loves you.

By 1970 I had my fifth child and my husband was drinking more and arguing. We argued a lot about church. He accused me of leaving the streets and other men, but now I chose God over him. I was a high school drop-out and I could not drive so I thought all I could do was have children. We tried birth control after the fifth child so I wasn't pregnant for a while. He would get drunk and call me names and sometimes hit me. The children were frightened and so I tried to keep him from being mad. I would turn my head if other men were around when we riding down the street. He would say "You're still a Ho, you just go to church." He would accuse me of going to the church to see someone. It was my church that gave me the courage and support to stay in church and raise my children. My biological sisters would tell me to leave him but I felt I owed him something for taking me back from the streets.

One night in 1972, my husband had come home drunk and the kids were in the bed sleep. There ages were 9, 6, 5, 4 and 2. He began to bring up the past and I was hoping he would get tired and fall asleep, but he didn't, he became violent with me and I ran outside in the backyard. I decided to go over to my mother's for a little while until he fell asleep. The kids were in bed and we had never had any problems with him waking them up before. I stayed over my mother's for an hour or more and then I figured he might be sleep by now. I sneaked back in the back door and hid in a small closet hoping to hear him snoring. I sat there a while until I heard what sounded like giggles, and I listed closely and it sounded like my nine year-old-daughter. I ran out of the backdoor around to the front of the house and called my daughter's name real loud and she quickly came out the door and my husband came staggering out behind her. I said to her "did he touch you" and she nodded yes.

I screamed "Run! Run!" And she quickly ran to me and I grabbed her hand and together we ran around the corner and there I saw a policeman who had stopped someone. I told him what I thought had happened and he put us in the car and took us home. By now another car had joined him and they shined the light on the house and told my husband to come out. He came staggering out and the police handcuffed him and took us back inside. They shinned the light on the couch and found some Vaseline and a flash light. They arrested him based on what my daughter said he did. This was a horrible experience because my daughter had to accuse her father of things which he denied. She was already hurt emotionally, although they found no evidence of penetration. They gave him a lighter sentence for pleading guilty to oral copulation which led to only five months served, three years' probation, and he must sign up as a sex-offender. (I don't think he ever did, they did not enforce it in those days).

During the time of his incarceration, he claimed salvation and asked for another chance. Neither I nor my pastor understood the depth of this problem. They went to court with me and encouraged me to take him back and be more careful to watch his behavior and keep praying. I thought it only happened because he was drunk. My sisters were against taking him back, but I was twenty-seven years old with five children and I didn't know what to do. I still felt I owed him a chance like he gave me.

So five months later he came home, and he was different, he did not go out any more and he did not drink. He would not go to church but he let me go more often. He took a course in computer programing and in 1973 my husband got a job for the county as a computer programmer. Life began to get better, we brought a new station wagon and he took us out on the weekends to Elysian Park and to Santa Monica pier. I was growing in the ministry and the pastor had recommended me for an Evangelist license. I started having bible study at home with the children in the evening after my husband went to work, since he worked from three to eleven in the evening. We moved nearer to his job but he still brought us back to the church and would go occasionally.

By 1976, when I was thirty, I was having my 6th child. I noticed that my husband tried to compensate for what he had done to our daughter by bringing her something every time he brought me something. It did make me a little jealous because I wanted to be special. We would even go to Disneyland on my daughter's birthday and I thought he was over doing it. If I ever even thought that something was amiss I would ask him if he was having any problems and he would deny it and I even asked my daughter to tell me it something like that happened again. I don't know if she thought I was helpless but she never said a word to me. My husband became more and more suspicious of our daughter when she was fifteen. He brought a pair of binoculars and one day insisted we go up to the school and spy on her. We finally went up to the High School and found her out of class. We took her home and he took her in the room to whip her. After he whipped her and left for work, she told me that the same thing that had happened when she was nine had happened ever since. I sent her to my friend's house from church because I thought the court was not the way to handle it.

My husband called back as he usually did to check on everything and I told him, that I knew what he had been doing. He came home and met with the pastor and wife and he cried and asked Jesus to come into his heart. My pastor's advice was sleep with my daughter. As I write this portion of the story it is the most difficult because I realize I failed as a mother. I should have left and never looked back, but I didn't. I was saved and filled with the Holy Ghost but I did not know how to handle this situation. I remember moving in with a girlfriend from the church but eventually I was back and pregnant again.

By late 1978 I was ready to deliver my seventh child and I decided to stay around the house a little longer since I had so much experience. I waited until the last minute and finally arrived at the hospital. They examined me and prepped me for the delivery and gave me the usual enema to make the delivery easier. They put me in a small bathroom in the delivery room so I would be ready for delivery. While in the bathroom, I felt a huge cramp that let me know this was more than a bowel movement. I knew the baby was coming so I stood up and opened the door and said "The baby is coming" and no sooner than the words came out of my mouth the baby slid out of me and landed on the floor. Doctors and nurses nearby ran over and laid me on a gurney. I remember signing something (maybe permission to treat the baby), but in a little while they told me that my baby had a hairline fracture but she would be alright. We wanted to sue the hospital but the lawyer said we did not have a case. We were grateful she was alright.

Six months later we bought our first house in Pasadena. My husband painted cartoons on the wall that led up stairs to the kid's room. He dug a trench in the back yard and planted large reed-like trees to give the impression of a swamp. The kids loved him because he was a boy at heart and would play games with them.

In 1980 I was pregnant with our eighth child, and I went to prenatal care at the Jackie Robinson Public health clinic and there I met a Registered Nurse who befriended me and one day she said "Laurie, you can do more than have children." I was thirty-five-years-old and believed that once you dropped out of High School your future was set. I did not know there was more. I had a little boy (our fourth) and my husband came to the hospital to visit before I was released. The hospital gave us a small bottle of Champaign to celebrate the birth of our child with a complimentary candlelight meal. He never opened the bottle and we placed it on the mantle. He had not taken a drink since 1972.

Not long after we were in Pasadena, my oldest daughter, started hanging out with a gang. She told her boyfriend about the sexual abuse and his mother, (a registered nurse) called the Department of Child Protective Services and they came and placed my children in foster homes. I was in cycle of abuse that I could not control. Someone from the outside had to step in and protect my children. The police went to my husband's job and arrested him, he was totally humiliated. They had placed the four girls in one foster home and the four boys in another. My oldest daughter, now seventeen, was placed separately and she expressed concern because they were all in different homes and the baby was not a year old.

They held my husband for a while and wanted to give him fifty years in prison, but the children and I walked out of court. It was difficult for a child to stand and accuse someone they love in court. Our daughter had requested that she be placed somewhere away from Pasadena where she was beginning to get in trouble. She wanted to keep her brothers and sisters together although she felt like she had to be sacrificed. I applied for Aid for Dependent Children since we had no other means of support and my husband was in jail. We were going to a church which was very supportive and I still believed my family would be saved. It wasn't long before my husband was released and returned home.

Soon I was pregnant with my ninth child and returned to the health clinic and saw the same nurse. She joked with me about being pregnant again and always tried to give me some good information about pregnancy and parenting. The pregnancy was uneventful and in July, 1981, I had my fifth son. The hospital gave us that same Champaign dinner and we took the bottle home and set it on the mantle with the other bottle. My husband could not find a job, and he would stay up all night working on gadgets and go to sleep in the early morning hours. He argued about me going to church and reminded me that I was the reason he lost his job.

My daughter had met a young man when she was in the foster home and they were married. They had an apartment in Palmdale. I decided to leave my husband in June once the kids were out of school and I moved in with my daughter. I got a job as a nursing assistant in a convalescent home and was certified after six months. It was so many of us that I knew I needed to be in my own place and when December arrived, I was ready to go back home for Christmas. There was the honeymoon phase of the cycle again and then the stressor "I had never been on his side from the beginning" and then the abuse. On New Year's Eve, 1982, he took the two Champaign bottles down off the mantle and began to drink again. That was ten years of sobriety by use of his sheer determination, rather than learning to live without alcohol.

I had learned to function with his accusations, by reading my bible and believing that God would deliver me some day. The girls were older and he began to get drunk and keep them up all night talking to them. We lost our home and found a smaller house. My husband had animosity toward my oldest son, and although he joined the band and did everything to please him, my husband was very harsh. Soon, my oldest son left and went to Palmdale to stay with his sister. Her home had become the safe place.

We were like soldiers; everyone did what they could to keep the peace. In 1984 I became pregnant with my tenth child (I believe I wanted ten children because my mother had ten) and I was flourishing at church. I could teach the bible and encourage others with my testimony but was still unable to deliver my family. When I look at it now, I believe every one of the children was born for a purpose, and that "All things work together for good, to them that love God, to them that all the called according to his purpose." (Romans 8:28)

One afternoon, I came home from a church service where God had used me to encourage other women, and my husband was drunk and harassing the family. He began to talk to my children and tell them negative things about me. I went in the backroom and began to cry, I felt totally helpless, I wanted to die. I went into the bathroom and got the bottle of aspirin and began to stuff handfuls in my mouth with some water. I lay down and in a little while I felt my ears closing up as if I were in a high altitude, I went in to tell my husband what I had taken. He took me in the bathroom and stuck his finger down my throat to induce vomiting. I felt the poison coming up but I still felt like my ears were stopped up.

He stopped being negative and later that evening a woman from the church came by. She said that she felt impressed to come over. I told her what I had just done and she prayed for me, that there would be no damage to my baby. You can be a Christian and still allow things to bring you low. There is a scripture that says "There hath no temptation (test) taken you but such as is common to man; but God is faithful, who will not suffer you to be tempted above that you are able; but will with the temptation also make a way of escape, that you may be able to bear it." 1 Corinthians 10:13

When I went to the clinic this time I knew it was my last time. I discussed permanent birth control or tubal ligation with the nurse. I had done my part in replenishing the earth. My husband did not want me to do this, but I was growing up. I was thirty-nine, there was a danger of having children at that age, and it was time to stop. I had allowed my husband to think of the majority of the children's names and some were named after him or by him. But this time I chose the name. I would name my last child after me. My last daughter was born in 1984. I was becoming more vocal about his treatment of the children and me. I knew things were coming to a head but I was not sure what to do. One day I was in the house cooking and my husband was outside drinking and I went to tell him something. I could not find him on the porch so I went to the side of the house and there I saw him. He had climbed up on the pipes and was looking in the bathroom window. I knew my second daughter was in the bathroom taking a bath. I was totally disgusted and it was like the light finally came on. I had to leave and never come back. I didn't know how, I didn't know when, but in my heart it was over. I sent my daughter to her sister's house where she finished high School.

I had decided I wasn't going to take it anymore. My sister's had always asked me how long was I going to let this happen and now I knew the answer. I moved into the front room and told him I was leaving as soon as I was able. It was not long after, I took my children to the pediatrician and they needed someone to help them. I told the doctor I was a certified nursing assistant (CNA) and I could take vital signs. I went back home and the next day I received a message from the doctor that I was hired. While I was working in the office, I found that there was a medical assisting program in the area and so I signed up. All of this was done without the permission of my husband. I was no longer bound by the very scriptures that had set me free. "Likewise, ye wives, be in subjection to your own husbands; that, if any obey not the word, they also may without the word be won by the conversation of the wife." (I Peter 3:1), and "wives submit yourselves unto your own husbands, as unto the Lord, for the husband is the head of the wife, even as Christ is the head of the church; and he is the savior of the body. Therefore, as the church is subject unto Christ, so let the wives be to their own husbands in everything." (Ephesians 5:22-24)

I went to the medical assisting program and met my friend Cynthia. She became an amazing asset in my life for this season. She had a little girl and I could tell her anything. She also had a car and could pick me up for school. I filed for divorce in 1986 and Cynthia served my husband. I soon left the doctor's office and got a job as a (CNA) to coincide with my school hours.

Salvation is a process that has in three parts; Justification, sanctification, and glorification. I was justified on January 8, 1967. Justified is a legal term signifying to acquit, declare righteous, show to be righteous. The scripture says "Therefore being justified by faith, we

have peace with God through our Lord Jesus Christ." (Romans 5:1)
I had been acquitted and declared righteous in God's court through
faith in the finished work of Jesus Christ on the cross. I was no longer
an enemy of God because of my sin, but there were things I needed
to learn from the scriptures, by "rightly dividing the word." In 2
Timothy 2:15 we are to "Study to show yourself approved unto God,
a workman that needeth not to be ashamed, rightly dividing the
word of truth." The word for "rightly dividing" is "orthotomounta"
which means to cut straight, it is to study diligently and apply the
word correctly to the situation. I was afraid of my husband, and afraid
of myself, and I used the scripture cover my fear. I would rather stay
with him and leave my children in harm's way than to trust God by
faith to take care of me and the children. For all of this I have been
forgiven. Thank you Lord.

Sanctification (hagiasmos) is a word that means a separation
from the world and its evils unto God and his righteousness. It is a
process whereby a believer through the study of and obedience to
the word of God "Lays aside every weight, and the sin which doth
easily beset us." (Hebrews 12:1b) We are admonished to "Put off the
old man (nature) with his deeds; and put on the new man (nature),
which is renewed in knowledge after the image of him that created
him." (Colossians 3:9-10)

PART 4

MIDDLE ADULT

STILL THIRSTY

During middle adulthood, we establish our careers, settle down within a relationship, begin our own families and develop a sense of being a part of the bigger picture. We give back to society through raising our children, being productive at work, and becoming involved in community activities and organizations. By failing to achieve these objectives, we become stagnant and feel unproductive. (4)

When God brought the children of Israel out of Egypt, it was not long before they complained to Moses "What shall we drink?" Gone was the glorious song that Miriam sang after the destruction of Pharaoh and his army in the Red Sea. They were focused only on their current lack. God was testing them to see if they would trust Him after such a mighty deliverance. (See Exodus 15:17-25). God had brought them out of Egypt and now He had to get Egypt out of them. You would think after all that God had brought me out of I would just move forward without looking back, but I found that I was still thirsty. This was 1986 and there was something that had been missing most of my life and that was love. It was what I craved even though I had suppressed it for the past nineteen years. I was forty-one years old and had a new found freedom and no one to hold me back. I had moved in with some church friends while I was saving for an apartment.

At the convalescent home, I met a man who was also a nursing assistant. I was attracted to him and as we worked together I found he had married a woman from the Philippines to give her a green card and that she worked in the same facility. After a few months of working with him we spent the night and I was ashamed to face the people who had took me in. We decided to move in together and I stopped going to church. This was what I feared. Those words I had heard for so long "You're still a Ho!" rang in my ears. There was one thing that was different I was not going back this time. I was going to live with my choices. We worked and lived together for a little while until I was fired for acting out at the job when I saw him with his wife. I was almost finished with the medical assisting program, when my boyfriend told me about being a registered nurse. He told me I could go to the city college and get my general education diploma (GED).

My girlfriend and I opted not to finish the computer portion of the medical assisting program, but to check into the college. I went to the Over Forty Agency and they helped me get another job at a beauty school. I was receiving welfare and my boyfriend knew a good thing. He had a major marijuana problem (he smoked it like people smoked cigarettes). I began to try it also. We moved to another apartment and I knew that if I kept smoking marijuana that I would not pass my classes.

One day, when my boyfriend was not at home, a couple of women came to my door and started talking about Jesus. One of them recognized me from another church and said she remembered my "testimony." I told them I was "In Love" and was not interested in going back to church. They told me of the church that was right around the corner. They left and I went on with my life. It was not long before one of the women returned to check on me again and I was still resistant. But something strange began to happen, on Sundays I didn't want to be "sexy for my age" any more but dressed in old house dresses. My boyfriend noticed and asked what was wrong. I told him I wanted to go back to church. He said "Go ahead, I'll be here when you get back." Each morning I would exercise to keep my stomach flat and during the exercise I wanted to pray for my children like I used to pray when I got up in the morning. But there was something I remembered from the bible that said "Now we know that God does not hear a sinner's prayer." (John 9:31) and "If I regard iniquity in my heart the Lord will not hear me." (Psalm 66:18). Here I was again taking God's word out of context. If God did not hear sinners no one would ever get saved. I did remember one scripture from Psalm 150:6 which says "Let everything that has breath praise the Lord." I began to praise the Lord that all of the kids were alright.

The adult children were on their own and I had five children with me; ages eleven, nine, seven, six, and three. I kept praising the Lord and getting more and more dissatisfied with my lifestyle. My boyfriend would always pick me up from the job although I would ride the bus to work and one night he was late. I caught the bus home and as I rode home I saw him heading toward the job. I hurried home and packed his clothes in some plastic bags and set them outside the door. He arrived shortly and began to knock. I told him to go away, and that I was going back to church. He was upset and said "Woman, I helped you. Just let me in to see if you got all of my clothes." I told him I would let him in but I had my hand on the phone and would call 911. I unlocked the chain on the door and ran to the phone. He went in the bedroom and stayed a while and then walked out. I locked the door. He went to the back of the building and threw a rock in the window. I went in the bedroom and looked in the closet and all of my clothes were cut with a knife. That could have been me.

It was 1988 and I went back to the church around the corner from my apartment that following Sunday with my children. I went to the altar and confessed to the Lord and I was reclaimed. I began to go to church regularly and God began to use me again giving my testimony and encouraging others. Soon after rededicating my life to Lord I ran into this man who had been giving me some problems. I would see him at various times and he would always try to pick me up but I didn't like him. I had worked at the beauty school when I was with the boyfriend and he would try to talk to me. He would stand outside and watch when my boyfriend came to pick me up. It was almost like everywhere I went I saw him. Well, I saw him again one day while I was on the way to the bank. He offered me a ride and I said to myself "I will tell him I am saved, and I don't want a boyfriend." So I accepted the ride to the bank and told him "I am saved now, I don't want a date and I go to church." He responded by saying "I know the Lord and Savior Jesus Christ and I go to Crenshaw Christian Center in Los Angeles." He did not tell me he was a licensed Baptist Minister, but I found that out later. I suspected he was trying to impress me, because I had never heard anyone call Jesus by all of those names. I invited him to my church and gave him my phone number. He called a couple of times but I hated his southern drawl when he would say "Hello Mam, I was just thinking about you." Irritating!

Jewel

Then he showed up at the church and got up in the Sunday morning service and introduced himself and said. "I really didn't come for anything but to meet this here lady. She looks like she needs some help." I was both flattered and embarrassed by that southern drawl. The kids made fun of it. This went on a few months, he came to church and called but I made excuses to avoid him. It was nearing Mother's Day and one of my daughters called to ask if she could take me to dinner. I told her I had someone who was interested in taking me to dinner and I would go with him. Mother's Day came and went and the southern gentleman did not call. I was mad. I missed a meal with my daughter because of him. Only he did not know I planned to go with him. He called one day, and I read the riot act. "Why didn't you call on Mother's Day? I missed going to dinner with my kids!" He responded, "I am sorry Mam, I had to usher that Sunday at Crenshaw Christian Center." He began to come over and take us to the park for a picnic. He joined the church and we began to talk about marriage. I received my GED and was admitted to the Vocational Nursing Program. I completed the program and became a Licensed Vocational nurse in 1989. He came to my graduation with flowers and all of the children came to the graduation. When they administrators called my name I could hear the children chant "Mama, Mama." I was so proud. God is the God of second chances.

Laurie's Picture of LVN

We were married in May of 1990. He had just brought a house with five bedrooms and a pool. I had enrolled in the registered nursing program at Pasadena City College. We drove to Las Vegas the same day I signed a prenuptial. I was reluctant to sign it but I did not want to get out of the will of God again after He had been so good to me. The prenuptial stated that the house was his and the white Cadillac was his, and the green car was mine (I had my own car). He went on to say in the document that the five adult children were not to come back home and the five younger children would not be adopted. I knew it was strange but I signed under duress because we were on the way to Las Vegas that same day. We didn't even stay, we drove back and we were already moved in (he had a house in the back by the pool).

Things were going well; I became a registered nurse in 1992. Our arguments consisted of his treatment of the children. The house had rooms added on with an extra kitchen, so that there were 3 bedrooms, a living room, a bathroom and a kitchen in the back portion of the house, and 2 bedrooms, a living room dining room, a kitchen, and a bathroom in the front portion of the house. There was a door in the closet that led to the other side of the house. I thought it was strange that my children lived in the back portion of the house and I came through the door that adjoined the houses when I was ready to go to bed. His premise was that they could relax better in their own place, and he wanted to keep the front part nice for visitors.

The oldest son at home was now 14, and nearly 6 feet tall. He felt like the protector of the family. They had more the one altercation. The children's father lived not too far way and sometimes that would cause conflict especially when my husband had to discipline my oldest son.

We went to church as a family. My children had bonded with the other children and the pastor and wife were very supportive of our family. My husband went to contractor's school and received his license. He also had a catering license, and leased a catering truck to sell barbecue. We gave family parties at the house and kids would swim. We were right down the street from a Christian after school program that really helped me with the children. I was able to excel in and out of the church. I enrolled in a program to receive my Bachelor's in Science. I received the degree and found that in just 18 months I could earn a Master's in Science of Nursing so I enrolled.

Bachelors Degree

We had our arguments (mostly about him putting my name on the house and his harshness with the children) as all blended families do but I was able to go Mississippi for his family reunion a few times. I knew that God had blessed me and I was thankful. I had lost my job as an instructor in early 1997 and I asked my son, who had just finished law school to come over to help me. My husband was jealous and upset because he considered himself a pseudo lawyer of sorts. I noted he had enrolled in Cal State trying to get a degree and had a complex related to education. He often told me that once I got my RN license that I was going to ride off on a Harley with a doctor.

Anyway, he started hollering at me in front of my son who was twenty-six years of age and my son walked up and hollered in his face these words; "How does it feel for someone to holler at you?" At that moment he was so mad, he told me to get out. It was not good for him to holler and get upset because of his high blood pressure. Two years earlier he had mentioned that while he was watering the grass all of a sudden, he felt numbness on the right side of his face and body. He went to the doctor and they told him he had a light stroke or a transient ischemic attack (TIA). I knew it was not good for him to argue so I told my son to leave. The next morning I was reading the bible when He came down stairs and he said" Let's go get some breakfast." I responded with "I thought you told me to get out?"

He answered, "I want you to get out but we can go have breakfast first." I had already found a place near one of my daughter's and when the mail man brought my last check from the job that day, I moved. The house was furnished and all I had to do was move in. I was not going back. This time I was not afraid, I was a nurse, I could get a job anywhere.

My three remaining children and I moved into the house in front of my third daughter. She had told me about the house and talked to the landlord and everything went smoothly. I decided not to communicate with my husband because he had asked me to leave before and when I did he was over every night. This time I wanted him to know that it was not alright to put me and my children out because he was "The landlord and the owner," as he used to say so often. I felt disrespected and humiliated and this time I did not believe that I deserved it. We were both Christians and we should have been able to pray together and work things out.

Satan has always hated marriage (as much as God hates divorce, because by bringing division in a home he causes the children to become confused. It is the seed that Satan wants to destroy, because of the potential, preachers, evangelists, and teachers we produce.

That's what the text in Malachi 2:14-16 is saying. I want you to understand it so I will use the amplified version:

"Yet you ask, why does He reject it? Because the Lord was witness [to the covenant made at your marriage] between you and the wife of your youth, against whom you have dealt treacherously and to whom you were faithless. Yet she is your companion and the wife of your covenant [made by your marriage vows]. And did not God make [you and your wife] one [flesh]? Did not One make you and preserve your spirit alive? And why [did God make you two] one? Because He sought a godly offspring [from your union]. Therefore take heed to yourselves, and let no one deal treacherously and be faithless to the wife of his youth. For the Lord, the God of Israel, says: I hate divorce and marital separation and him who covers his garment [his wife] with violence. Therefore keep a watch upon your spirit [that it may be controlled by My Spirit], that you deal not treacherously and faithlessly [with your marriage mate]."

These scriptures show why the divorce rate in the church is as high as it is in the world. Christians judge their mates by the standards of the world; Are they working, do they make me feel good, are they pleasing to look at, can they give me what I want. We need to walk in the Spirit when it comes to our mates so that we can produce children that will bring glory to God.

That was the last I heard from my husband for a while. I stayed busy working full time, finishing my Master's degree, and going to church. One day he called me and told me about something that had happened to him. He was driving on a one-way-street going the wrong way, literally. He didn't know what had happened but he heard God speaking to him saying; "You did not treat your wife right, you need to put her name on the house, join the church where she goes, you need to give those three children $500 each and giver your wife $5,000, then you can renew your vows." He also told me that God told him to "Cry out to Him." I actually heard him crying out one time upstairs in his bedroom praying after that. This was remarkable! He told everyone, and my daughter and son-in-law actually taped his testimony.

He still didn't want me to move back in the house because he was having it changed into a boarding house with eight bedrooms that could be rented out. He said we would buy another house together. He picked me up one day and took me to the Real Estate Broker and had my name placed on the deed to his house. Our next stop was Union Bank where he transferred $5,000 into my account and we opened an account for each of the children with $500 deposited in each account. At the end of the day he was exhausted, he did not want me to stay with him, he just took me home. It was as if he got something heavy off of his back. We joined Victory Full Gospel Bible Church under the leadership of Bishop James Henry. He welcomed us into the ministry. On Wednesday night of the same week, Bishop Henry asked each of the ministers to pray for something. We all prayed for various issues but my husband prayed for the Bishop, his health and well-being.

On Friday, July 30, 1997, we decided to go to Los Angeles and get some fish at our favorite place on Imperial. We bought his favorite fish, ate at the place and came home. That night he suffered a major stroke and I called the paramedics and they rushed him to the hospital. After the CAT scan, the neurologist told me that the brain had been damaged by a "Pontine bleed" at the base of the brain and it was irreversible and I had 72 hours to make the decision to take him off of the ventilator. The doctor told me that he would never regain consciousness because of the area of the brain that was affected. They could keep him alive for about a year on the ventilator but the complications from pneumonia, bed sores, and contractures would increase.

As a registered nurse, I looked at the chart and saw the prognosis written by the physician, and, although family members were watching the vital signs on the life support machines expecting recovery, I knew how serious it was. I called Bishop Henry and asked him what I should do. He calmly asked "What is God saying to you?" I thought about my husband, how proud he was and he would never want to be in this condition. I thought about his recent confession of faith to everyone and knew what I had to do. I responded to Bishop Henry "God is saying, I came that you might have life and that more abundantly, and it is time to release him."

This was the person who had given me self-worth, this was the one that taught me I was important, and this was the man who came into my life to help me. He would always say "You're gonna miss me." Wow! It was like I was hit in my stomach and all of the wind was knocked out. I began to think of how I could have done better as a wife as I went through the grief process. I was angry that God took him so soon, but I realized that God does not make mistakes. We had two beautiful services and the Bishop did the Eulogy, recalling that my husband had chosen to pray for him when everyone else was praying for other things. (The following year the Bishop died while standing in the pulpit preaching.) The second service was held in my husband's home church in Mississippi.

I called my son, who was studying to take the bar, to come in and handle the paperwork regarding the house and the mortgage. I did not know what to do. The lien holders came to appraise the house and found that the alterations that had been made were not according to code, which took away from the value of the house. My husband had cashed in his life insurance and I needed the money to pay for funeral costs and transporting him back to Mississippi. I was finishing the Master's program and working but I needed the support of my family, so I invited some of my children to move in and pay rent. This was a big mistake as they bickered over who was the greatest and no one wanted to pay anything. We finally lost the house and I moved to Monrovia.

Master's Graduation

I thought of myself as a strong Christian as long as I had my husband, my home, and my church but these were all things that made me appear strong. God is always asking us for our total surrender and most believe they have done that until the props are removed. I cannot blame anyone for the bad decisions I made after my husband's passing. The old issues which seemed to be gone suddenly surfaced again. It is important for Christians not to be too harsh on others when they fail because we are all capable of falling. That's why the scripture reminds us in Galatians 6:1 "Brethren, if a man be overtaken in a fault, ye which are spiritual, restore such an one in the spirit of meekness; considering thyself, lest thou also be tempted." Once our safety nets are removed, i.e., job, titles, husband, wife, children, etc., we tend to regress. No wonder the word says

"Wherefore let him that thinketh he standeth take heed lest he fall." (I Corinthians 10:12

My daughter wanted me to meet her boyfriend's father who was a minister. I rejected the idea for a while until I received a phone call. We talked over the phone a few times until curiosity got the best of me. We met and I was impressed as he played the piano and spoke about ministry. He had nine children who were all adult, he was waiting for his next assignment as a pastor, and he was coming out of a relationship, we had several things in common. I was a widow of only a few months, and should have been aware of my vulnerability, but I really didn't stop to think. It wasn't long before I committed myself to the relationship. He was given a pastorate shortly after we met and I became a member of the Methodist church. It was in this church that I acknowledged my call to ministry and began the process of becoming licensed and ordained. I was asked to preach a trial sermon before the church and any invited guest. After the trial sermon, one of the elders took a seat next to me and asked "How did you learn the bible so well?" I guess this meant I did a good job. I received my license to preach at the quarterly conference. Now I was able to assist the pastor in the reading of the scriptures and prayer.

My expectations for this relationship never came to fruition, although I labored tirelessly to make it happen. I stayed there for two years and as I realized the relationship was coming to an end I received a call from an older female pastor in another city to come and help her. I must be honest; I really didn't want to go, because I felt as if I was being sent to the desert by the pastor to get rid of me. I finally made up my mind to go. I started off living with my son until I was able to find a job as a Director of Nursing. I was able to use my past experience and the wisdom of God to help start the school's vocational nursing program. Soon I was in my own place and my children and grandchildren who lived in the area were attending the church. The bible says "The steps of a good man are ordered by the Lord; and he delighteth in his way." (Psalms 37:23) This simply means that God orders and establishes the details of His children's lives. We might have intentions to find a husband, to answer someone's call, or even to get away from a problem but God is in the midst. When Moses killed the Egyptian and fled to the backside of the desert, it was all in the plan of God. (See Exodus 2:11-22).

The failures of those in leadership should not surprise us when we are acutely aware of our own failures. Leaders must with stand both adversity and prosperity. The scripture reminds that we are tested by both in Proverbs 30:8-9. Sometimes we believe the hype we receive related to our gifting, ability or talent. We forget to pray, study the word, and bring our bodies under subjection (I Corinthians 9:27). That is a set up for failure, and when something devastating happens, we try to find relief through relationships, alcohol or even drugs. Yes, Christians return like pigs to their own vomit, but even while the smell of vomit is still on our breath the Lord reaches out to remind us that he is our satisfying portion. (See Luke 15:11-24). There have been Christians who were formally drug addicts and when a crisis came they resorted to their old craving. Those of us who never had that craving, decided or judged that they were not saved. My drug of choice was the "pursuit of love" and I was still looking.

The new church and new congregation was helpful for me to refocus on ministry. It was a joy to pastor my children and grandchildren. This female pastor in her seventies had founded this church in the desert. She was given an appointment and she went out and rented a Masonic Hall. It was the perfect price and the perfect place. We had ample parking and the use of the folding chairs. I would arrive every Sunday morning and set up the chairs. It was there I learned to be faithful to the ministry. It was there I learned to follow leadership no matter what I thought about her decisions. I remember one Sunday morning getting upset with the pastor because she had embarrassed my son who wanted to be a local preacher. I don't even remember what it was all about but I remember her words "You may not like the way I do things, but you have to come by me to be ordained." She was on the ordination committee and she could tell them I was not ready and they would accept her observation.

Ten children

I stayed there four years and with the support of the pastor I was encouraged to write my thesis and present it to the Seminary with which she was associated. I received an Honorary Doctorate in Sacred Ministry with her support and encouragement from Reed Western Theological Seminary. Later in the same year 2004, I was ordained an Elder in the African Methodist Episcopal Zion Church. This pastor educated, instructed, and nurtured me to become all I could be and I will never forget her.

When the boyfriend-pastor left me out in the cold, I quickly gravitated to the Elder who had heard my trial sermon and who thought I had potential. I had never given him a thought before, in fact, I thought he was quite arrogant as he taught "The School of the Prophets" at the annual conference. I had seen his name in the "Book of Discipline" and I believed he was somebody. I remember calling him one evening, while attending an affair with the church, and telling him how devastated I was because my pastor had brought his new girlfriend to the banquet. I still remember his words of spiritual wisdom and compassion "Why don't you come over here and we can have our own banquet?" All of my life I had wanted a father, a spiritual guide or a leader, that would help me through my problems. I found that a woman must trust her heavenly father, who alone, is able to lead and to guide. The Elder and I began to converse by phone and go on dinner dates even though he lived in Los Angeles and I lived in Lancaster.

The school where I was employed as Director of Nursing wanted to open a second campus in Ventura and I decided to move and help get the Vocational Nursing Program started. I moved to Oxnard in 2004. Not many months later the pastor who had trained me and helped me become ordained passed away.

I looked in the phone directory and found a African Methodist Episcopal Church in the area. The Elder and I had been discussing marriage for a while and in February of 2005 we were married. "At Last" was the song that was playing over and over in the little chapel in downtown Los Angeles. We filled out all of the paperwork and paid the money and that was it. No fanfare; just a commitment I had made within my heart as we conversed via e-mail from the book of Ruth. "Entreat me not to leave thee, or to return from following after thee, for wither thou goest I will go, and where thou lodgest, I will lodge, thy people shall be my people and thy God my God. Where thou diest will I die and there will I be buried; the Lord do so to me and more also, if ought but death part me and thee." (Ruth 1: 16-17.

Dr. McDonald and Me

PART 5

SENIOR LIFE

As we grow older and become senior citizens, we tend to slow down our productivity, and explore life as a retired person. It is during this time that we contemplate our accomplishments and are able to develop integrity if we see ourselves as leading a successful life. If we see our lives as unproductive, feel guilt about our pasts, or feel that we did not accomplish our life goals, we become dissatisfied with life and develop despair, often leading to depression and hopelessness. (5)

As I look back over my life there are some things I am proud of and there some things of which I am ashamed. But there is no condemnation as I have taken each of my failures to the cross of Christ. He is my great High Priest who intercedes on my behalf. His death has atoned for my sin. Jesus is the priest, the sacrifice, and the reason why I live a fulfilled life.

I had finally realized the true meaning of love. The definition is portrayed in I Corinthians 13:4-7 "Love is patient, love is kind. It does not envy, it does not boast, it is not proud. It does not dishonor others, it is not self-seeking, it is not easily angered, it keeps no record of wrongs. Love does not delight in evil but rejoices with the truth. It always protects, always trusts, always hopes, always perseveres." What I had been seeking was an elusive emotion that falls and rises with the tide. What I found was commitment, an act of sacrifice and acceptance. I fell in love with the Elder's mind because I always admired his ability to quickly quote the appropriate text whenever he was teaching, but I'll be here when he can't remember who I am. He is a quiet and reserve man and I am outspoken. He is contemplative and I usually act and then think, but God is gracious. We don't argue or fight, we realize that God is a God of mercy and grace and he didn't have to bless but He did.

When the school where I was employed, wanted to expand to the Riverside area, we moved to San Bernardino and began attending an African Methodist Episcopal Church in June of 2006. There was a new pastor at the church but he readily received us, and I became the Director of the Women's Ministry.

In 2008 I was asked by the pastor if I would take a preaching engagement in Victorville. My husband and I went and found a small group of people worshipping in the Community Center. They were very congenial to my husband and I and I thought the service went well. Not long after this, I received a call from the Presiding Elder, stating that the church requested that I become their pastor. I discussed this with my husband and he felt that it would be too much for me driving to Moreno Valley where the new school was located. I spoke to my pastor and he described the situation in detail. The church had had 5 pastors in 6 years and were fragmented, disappointed, and only 8 members remained. I considered all of the facts and was leaning toward passing this one by until I heard the report from the pastor who supplied the church for 1 year.

When the Bishop asked where the people were she responded "They are discouraged." She described the area, the few remaining members and the almost impossibility of sustaining a church under those conditions. As I heard her report I also heard the Holy Spirit say to me "They are sheep without a shepherd." I knew then and there that God was calling me to Victorville. I was appointed on the last day of the Annual Conference.

I moved to Victorville from San Bernardino and we began having bible study in the homes and meet in Community Center on

Sunday. One of the members worked for a Broadcasting Company and needed to fill radio program slots and I wanted to get the gospel out and help her at the same time. This radio/internet broadcast goes into two prisons, throughout the Victor Valley area and around the world. By 2010 our church moved into our rented facility and all of their furniture was out of storage. We began to grow as former members returned and others joined. I am proud to have been sent back as pastor for the past 3 years.

The stages of Development have all been accomplished in my life except old age. I have the comfort of the scriptures that God will not abandon me because I am not as productive as I use to be. Read Psalm 71:5-18 "For you have been my hope, O Sovereign LORD, my confidence since my youth. From birth I have relied on you; you brought me forth from my mother's womb. I will ever praise you. I have become like a portent to many, but you are my strong refuge. My mouth is filled with your praise, declaring your splendor all day long. Do not cast me away when I am old; do not forsake me when my strength is gone. For my enemies speak against me; those who wait to kill me conspire together. They say, "God has forsaken him; pursue him and seize him, for no one will rescue him." Be not far from me, O God; come quickly, O my God, to help me. May my accusers perish in shame; may those who want to harm me be covered with scorn and disgrace. But as for me, I will always have hope; I will praise you more and more. My mouth will tell of your righteousness, of your salvation all day long, though I know not its measure. I will come and proclaim your mighty acts, O Sovereign LORD; I will proclaim your righteousness, yours alone. Since my youth, O God, you have taught me, and to this day I declare your marvelous deeds. Even when I am old and gray, do not forsake me, O God, till I declare your power to the next generation, your might to all who are to come." I am sure that He that has begun a good work in me will perform it and that Jesus Christ is able to save us to the uttermost, all the way to the grave, because he continues to live at the right hand of the Father to make intercession for us. Praise God from Whom all blessings flow!

1-5 Mcleod, S. A. (2008). *Simply Psychology; Erik Erikson | Psychosocial Stages.* Retrieved 16 January 2012, from http://www.simplypsychology.org/Erik-Erikson.html